THE ANCIENT
Maya

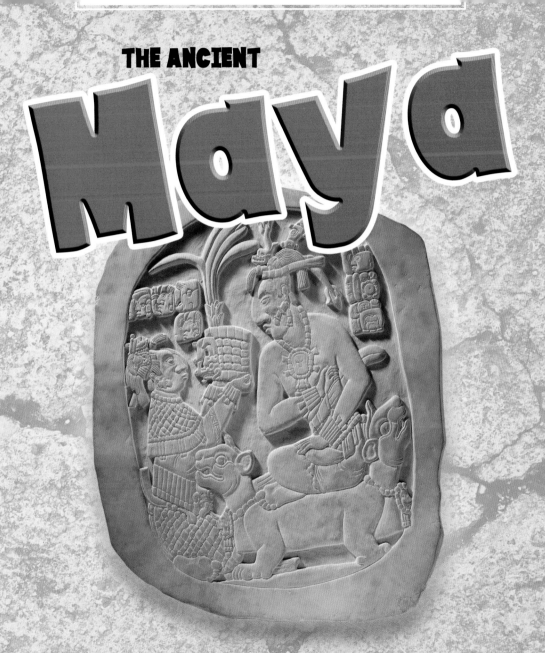

Louise Spilsbury

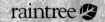
raintree
a Capstone company — publishers for children

Raintree is an imprint of Capstone Global Library Limited, a company incorporated in England and Wales having its registered office at 264 Banbury Road, Oxford, OX2 7DY – Registered company number: 6695582

www.raintree.co.uk
myorders@raintree.co.uk

Text © Capstone Global Library Limited 2020
The moral rights of the proprietor have been asserted.

Original illustrations © Capstone Global Library Limited 2020
Originated by Capstone Global Library Ltd
Printed and bound in India

ISBN 978 1 4747 7735 3 (hardback)
23 22 21 20 19
10 9 8 7 6 5 4 3 2 1

ISBN 978 1 4747 7740 7 (paperback)
24 23 22 21 20
10 9 8 7 6 5 4 3 2 1

British Library Cataloguing in Publication Data
A full catalogue record for this book is available from the British Library.

Acknowledgements
We would like to thank the following for permission to reproduce photographs: Cover: Shutterstock: Vadim Petrakov; Inside: Shutterstock: Anton Ivanov: p. 28; Asanru: p. 10; Igor Dymov: p. 13; Gabriele Fabrizio: pp. 30-31b; Lukiyanova Natalia Frenta: p. 19; Diego Grandi: p. 4; Gresei: p. 27; Lev Levin: p. 15; Vaclav Mach: p. 22; W. Scott McGil: p. 25; MNStudio: p. 39; Nikidel: p. 12; Volodymyr Nikitenko: p. 29; Leon Rafael: pp. 1, 35; Dr Morley Read: p. 23; Dmitry Rukhlenko: p. 11; Jose Ignacio Soto: p. 40; Shane W Thompson: pp. 30-31t; Paul Vowles: p. 41; Yummyphotos: pp. 32-33b; Wikimedia Commons: pp. 33, 34; Authenticmaya: p. 8b; Simon Burchell: p. 38; El Comandante: pp. 8-9t; Daderot: p. 21; Carlos Delgado: p. 26; FA2010: pp. 6-7t; John Hill: p. 24; Inakiherrasti: p. 37; Adam Jones: p. 5; LACMA; The Proctor Stafford Collection, purchased with funds provided by Mr. and Mrs. Allan C. Balch: p. 18; Leonard G.: p. 16; Sainterx: pp. 36, 45; Wolfgang Sauber: pp. 14, 20; SiMeCalS: pp. 6-7b; Lewis Spence: p. 17; Pavel Vorobiev: p. 43; Michel Wal: p. 42.
Design Elements by Shutterstock.

Every effort has been made to contact copyright holders of material reproduced in this book. Any omissions will be rectified in subsequent printings if notice is given to the publisher.

CONTENTS

CHAPTER 1

The mysterious Maya

The Maya developed an advanced **civilization** that reached its peak from about AD 300 to AD 900. At one point, the Maya ruled over a huge area almost 517,998 square kilometres (200,000 square miles) wide, which included parts of what are now southern Mexico, Guatemala, Belize, Honduras and El Salvador. The Maya were the first in the region to develop a highly sophisticated **culture** with art, science, fine buildings and a system of writing.

Early Maya

Between about 1200 BC and AD 300, the Maya were just one of several different cultures that lived in the region. The early Maya moved around, often with small herds of animals. Then they became farmers, who learned how to grow crops such as maize, squash, beans and chilli peppers. They also hunted and fished. They started to live in small villages near rivers, which supplied them with fresh water. This enabled them to grow more food for their families and to settle down in one place all year round.

A HIDDEN CULTURE

Maya culture remained a mystery for many years, partly because its cities were nestled away among tall rainforest trees.

Rise of the city-states

With plentiful food to feed increasing numbers of hungry mouths as populations grew, some small villages began to grow to form cities in the coastal lowlands and rainforests of the regions. Most Maya cities were built in patches of thick jungle, which meant they were hidden from view. Over time, the different cities and their surrounding areas and villages came under the rule of powerful kings. They became **city-states**, each ruled by a different king and royal family. Often, these city-states were very violent and went to war against each other. Even though they were never united under one ruler, all Maya shared a common culture and religion.

5

Powerful city-states

At one point in Maya history, there were around 40 different Maya city-states, each with a different ruler and up to 50,000 inhabitants. Most of the cities at the centre of these city-states were laid out in a similar way. The king's palace was in the centre as were the giant **pyramids** and **temples** used for worship. There was also a plaza (square) near the centre. This was used for markets and meetings, and the other buildings spread out around it.

Ruling the city-states

Rulers of the city-states **inherited** their right to rule from their fathers. Maya kings had the right to rule over everyone else in a city-state for life. A new king came to power only after the old king died, when his son or brother took over, or when a new ruling family conquered the city in battle. Battles between Maya cities were common. Sometimes a woman ruled over a city-state, if the king died and his son was not old enough to take over, or if the king was away at war.

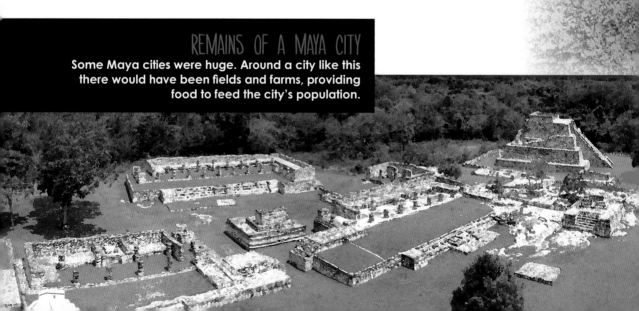

REMAINS OF A MAYA CITY

Some Maya cities were huge. Around a city like this there would have been fields and farms, providing food to feed the city's population.

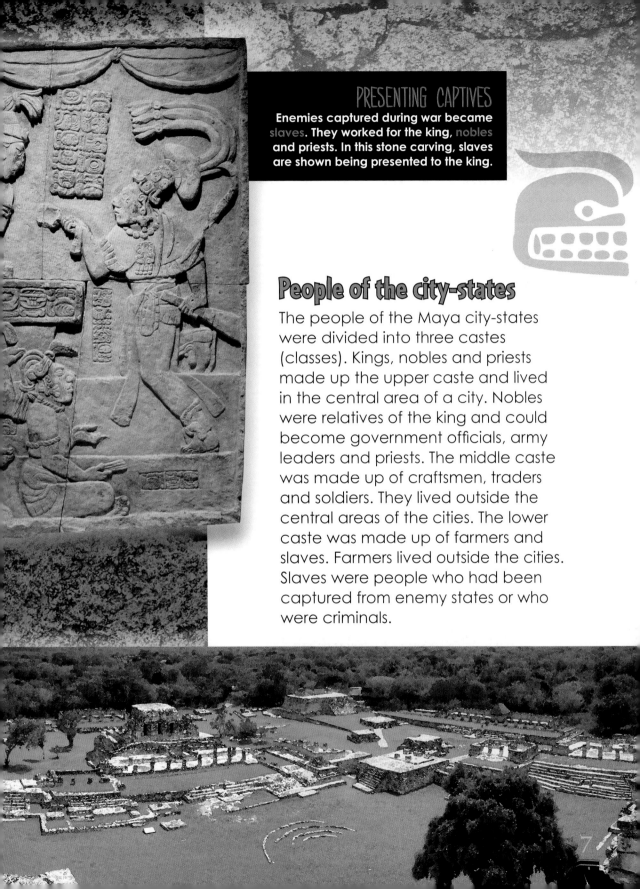

People of the city-states

The people of the Maya city-states were divided into three castes (classes). Kings, nobles and priests made up the upper caste and lived in the central area of a city. Nobles were relatives of the king and could become government officials, army leaders and priests. The middle caste was made up of craftsmen, traders and soldiers. They lived outside the central areas of the cities. The lower caste was made up of farmers and slaves. Farmers lived outside the cities. Slaves were people who had been captured from enemy states or who were criminals.

Examining evidence

There are many different types of evidence that hold clues to the lives of the ancient Maya. Archaeologists are people who study ancient cultures and use the evidence they find to piece together the mysteries of the past.

Some of these remains of the past are big and easily seen, such as the ruins of ancient cities and their temples and palaces. Archaeologists who study the ancient Maya also find clues in smaller items, such as ancient writings and artefacts, that they may find buried underground or hidden in **tombs**. Artefacts are pots, weapons, masks, carvings and other items that can tell us about the past. Sometimes archaeologists find artefacts, but builders or farmers can also find artefacts when they are digging up an area of land.

THE LARGEST PALACE

In 1967, students from Harvard University discovered the ruins of Cancuén, the largest palace in the Maya world. On a wall in one of its 200 rooms was this panel showing an ancient Maya ruler called Tajal Chan Ahk.

ANALYSE THE ANCIENTS

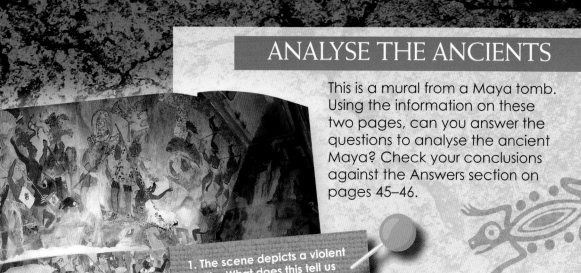

This is a mural from a Maya tomb. Using the information on these two pages, can you answer the questions to analyse the ancient Maya? Check your conclusions against the Answers section on pages 45–46.

1. The scene depicts a violent battle. What does this tell us about the ancient Maya?

2. The scene shows warriors using weapons. How do paintings such as this help archaeologists to work out that stone tips were used on spears, even though the wooden spear poles rotted away long ago?

One reason we know so much about the ancient Maya is that they developed a complex system of writing and used it to record some aspects of their lives. They also made sculptures that show us what they wore and what animals lived alongside them. Early ideas about Maya life suggested they were a peaceful people. The discovery of weapons such as stone spear tips, warrior masks and tomb murals (wall paintings) depicting scenes of battle contradicted these theories, however. They showed kings raiding other cities to capture enemies, or to take land or valuable goods. The paintings show that Maya warriors painted their bodies, sometimes like the coats of dangerous animals, to make them seem more fierce, before going to war.

CHAPTER 2

Master builders

The Maya were skilled builders and **architects**. They designed and built palaces, temples, pyramids and homes, many of which can still be seen today. The cities were linked by well-built roads that carved paths through the rainforests and jungles. The most distinctive buildings in most cities were the towering pyramids.

Different pyramids

Religion was at the centre of the Maya's lives, and pyramids were their most important religious buildings. The Maya built two different types of pyramids. They were both the same shape: square at the bottom, rising and narrowing to a high, flat top. The top was flat so that a temple could be built on it. One type of pyramid had steps that were designed to be climbed. Priests would climb to the top of the temple and perform ceremonies. The pyramids were built high up so the priests would be closer to the gods above. The second type of pyramid had steps that were too steep and were not meant to be climbed. These pyramids were considered **sacred.**

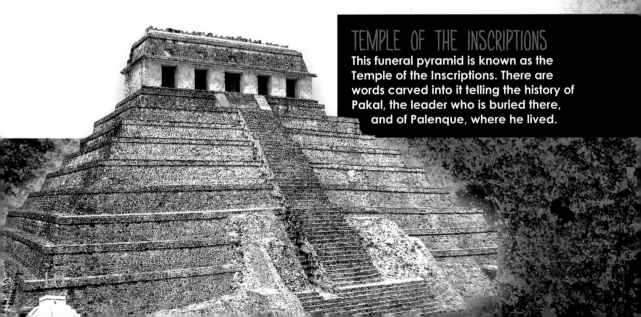

TEMPLE OF THE INSCRIPTIONS
This funeral pyramid is known as the Temple of the Inscriptions. There are words carved into it telling the history of Pakal, the leader who is buried there, and of Palenque, where he lived.

Pyramid purposes

As well as being used for religious ceremonies, the Maya pyramids served other purposes. The pyramids were so tall that they rose above even the highest trees in the rainforest. This reminded people that the gods were always watching over them. It also allowed people to use the pyramids as landmarks to find cities otherwise hidden within the thick jungles.

ANALYSE THE ANCIENTS

This is an ancient Maya pyramid. Using the information you have read, can you answer the questions to analyse the ancient Maya?

1. The pyramid has a flat top with a building on it. What do you think this building was used for?

2. The pyramid and the building on top are very high up. Why do you think the ancient Maya built their temples so tall?

Palenque palace

One of the best examples of Maya building is the Royal Palace of Palenque, in what is today the state of Chiapas, Mexico. It is believed that King Pakal the Great, who ruled from AD 615 to AD 683, and his sons owned it.

Places of power

Palaces such as Palenque were usually the largest buildings in a city. Palenque is several storeys high. It was 91 metres (300 feet) by 73 m (240 ft). Its square, four-storey tower was 24 m (80 ft) high. Palenque and other palaces were very big because they were not just places where the king lived. They were also the headquarters of the city, from where the whole city-state was run. There were rooms for meetings, and places where officials lived and worked, helping the king make decisions about wars, trade and festivals, for example.

RUINS OF PALENQUE
This tall, stepped pyramid has a central stairwell leading up to the temple at the top. It is one of the oldest buildings in Palenque.

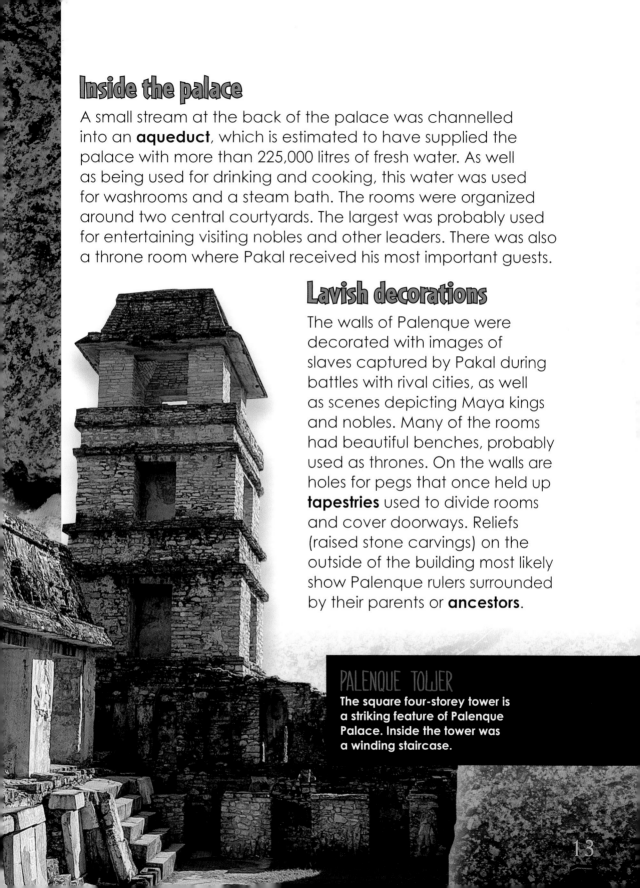

Inside the palace

A small stream at the back of the palace was channelled into an **aqueduct**, which is estimated to have supplied the palace with more than 225,000 litres of fresh water. As well as being used for drinking and cooking, this water was used for washrooms and a steam bath. The rooms were organized around two central courtyards. The largest was probably used for entertaining visiting nobles and other leaders. There was also a throne room where Pakal received his most important guests.

Lavish decorations

The walls of Palenque were decorated with images of slaves captured by Pakal during battles with rival cities, as well as scenes depicting Maya kings and nobles. Many of the rooms had beautiful benches, probably used as thrones. On the walls are holes for pegs that once held up **tapestries** used to divide rooms and cover doorways. Reliefs (raised stone carvings) on the outside of the building most likely show Palenque rulers surrounded by their parents or **ancestors**.

PALENQUE TOWER

The square four-storey tower is a striking feature of Palenque Palace. Inside the tower was a winding staircase.

13

Building the cities

The magnificent buildings of the Maya cities were built at a time when there were no cranes or machines to help construct them. It took thousands of men, working with their hands and simple tools, to complete them.

Metals were not common in the area, so the Maya used tools made of stone, wood and shells. The king and priests decided how the temples and palaces would look. They then instructed and supervised the members of the lowest caste to build them. The farmers and slaves worked on these construction projects to show their respect for the king, or because they were forced to. Most building work took place after harvests, during the time when there was little to be done on the farms. Workers had to carry stone and other materials on their backs or roll them on logs to move them to the building site from the **quarry** or other sources. Then they chipped and hacked away at the stone to make it into the shapes needed for the buildings.

CARVED IN STONE
The outside of many Maya temples and palaces were covered with decorative carvings like this one.

MANY MASKS

The most famous building at the Maya city of Kabah is the "Palace of the Masks". The exterior is decorated with hundreds of stone masks of a long-nosed Maya god called Chac.

The homes of the lowest-caste families were on the outskirts of the city or in the countryside beyond. They usually consisted of one room. There was usually a separate hut for cooking and washing. There were often several houses together, belonging to different members of the same family, around one central yard. Houses were built on platforms of stone or earth to prevent them being flooded in heavy rains. The houses had walls made from branches covered in clay. A simple sloping roof was made from palm tree leaves. Unlike the stone palaces and temples, most of these structures rotted away long ago.

CHAPTER 3

Maya beliefs

The ancient Maya believed in hundreds of different gods. They believed that these gods were all-powerful and controlled everything that happened on Earth.

Maya gods

Most of the Maya gods were linked to nature. There were Sun gods, rain gods and gods for thunder and lightning, for example. Ah Mun was the god of maize (corn) one of the most important Maya crops. Chac was the rain god who watered the crops. Huracán was the god of the wind, and his name is where today's word "hurricane" comes from. Itzamna ruled the sky and was one of the gods whom the Maya believed created Earth. He is usually considered the chief god, and according to Maya legend, he invented writing. The gods could change themselves into human or animal shapes or a combination of the two.

MAYA SUN GOD

This is an ancient terracotta image of the Maya Sun god, Ah K'in, who was often shown as an old man with a hooked nose. He was believed to control drought and disease.

Pleasing the gods

The gods could be good, but they could also be evil. When something bad happened, such as lightning, a storm or a drought, the Maya thought that this was a sign that the gods were angry with them. They tried hard to keep the gods happy. They built temples in their honour and filled them with beautiful carvings. Priests carried out ceremonies and **rituals** to keep the gods happy. The Maya believed their priests could communicate with the gods through such ceremonies, making Maya priests very important and powerful. Maya kings were the most important priests. They were seen as the link between humans and gods. When the kings died, they were thought to became gods themselves.

Three worlds

The Maya believed that the world was divided into three main parts: the upper world of heaven, the middle world of Earth and the underworld. They thought the three different parts were connected by a giant world tree. Heaven was believed to have 13 layers, and each layer had its own god. The underworld had nine layers, with nine evil gods, and was linked with the sea.

MAYA GODS
This image from a Maya vase shows a procession of Maya gods.

Sacrifices and ceremonies

The priests and kings communicated with gods in ceremonies and rituals. These included noisy, colourful festivals and sacrificial **bloodletting** rituals.

Festivals

Festivals to honour the many Maya gods were held every 20 days in cities. The priests wore costumes and danced on the steps of the temple, where huge crowds could watch them. There were also ritual dances and singing. Large seashells were used as trumpets to create music. These shells were rare and valuable in cities far from the ocean. The Maya also believed that the sea was connected to the gods and the underworld. In these ceremonies, kings and nobles often entered a trance, as though they were communicating with the gods. These events helped prove that the king was a godlike and powerful figure.

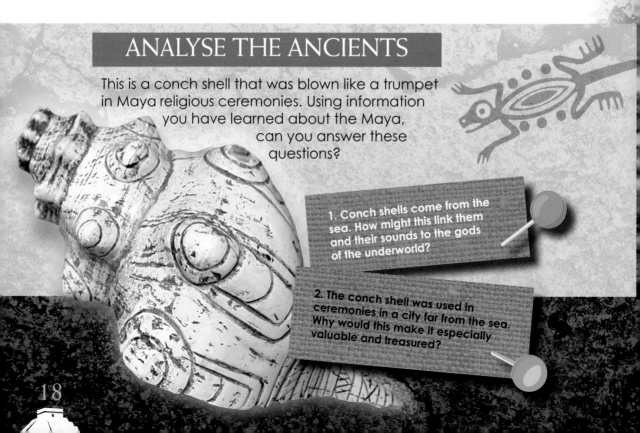

ANALYSE THE ANCIENTS

This is a conch shell that was blown like a trumpet in Maya religious ceremonies. Using information you have learned about the Maya, can you answer these questions?

1. Conch shells come from the sea. How might this link them and their sounds to the gods of the underworld?

2. The conch shell was used in ceremonies in a city far from the sea. Why would this make it especially valuable and treasured?

HUMAN SACRIFICIES

The skulls of people who had been sacrificed were often piled outside temples on racks. Outer temple walls sometimes had stone carvings of these racks.

Offerings of blood

For the Maya, **offerings** of blood were vital to keep the gods happy. This sometimes took the form of bloodletting, in which a king used a knife or the sharp spine of a stingray, to cut his skin and drop blood into a bowl. Kings' wives sometimes pulled a rope with thorns through their tongue to draw blood. Paper was soaked in blood, then burned to send it to the gods. Animals such as turkeys, dogs, squirrels, quail and lizards were **sacrificed** on top of the pyramids. Sometimes, human prisoners of war and slaves were killed in sacrifice, too. One of the sacrifices to the rain god Chac was to drown children in wells.

The afterlife

The Maya believed that after anyone died, they went to an **afterlife** in the underworld. If people survived this dangerous place and the demons there, they could then make their way up to heaven where they would find peace and happiness forever.

Offerings for the afterlife

Some Maya people buried their dead under plazas or in special pits. Others put the bones of their relatives in stone containers called urns and left them in caves. When most people died, they were wrapped in a simple cloth and buried beneath the floor of their house. This meant that for most people, the house they lived in was both a home and a tomb. Alongside the body, people buried the dead person's important belongings. They put maize in their mouth to feed them on their trip to the underworld. The Maya made regular offerings to their ancestors. They believed having their ancestors nearby meant they could watch over them and hopefully help keep them safe. If a house was falling apart and was abandoned, the Maya would treat it with the same respect as a tomb.

BURIED IN A MASK

This death mask of King Pakal was made from hundreds of pieces of a green stone called jade. It was found covering his face when archaeologists opened his tomb at Palenque.

This beautiful burial urn dates from AD 400 to AD 600 and was used to hold the remains of someone important. The person was either placed in the urn as a tightly wrapped bundle, or their bones were put in it a while after death.

A king's death

Maya kings were believed to become gods after they died. They were put to rest in special tombs, often under their palaces or pyramids. Their faces were often covered in special death masks. These were usually made from a special and rare green stone called jade, which was of religious importance to the Maya. The Maya often placed jade beads in the mouth of the dead for the same reason. The Maya believed that the expensive and elaborate death masks would prove to the gods that the king was important, so they would accept him as one of their own. The kings' tombs were filled with rich burial gifts for him to use in the afterlife.

CHAPTER 4

Work and trade

There were many different jobs in the time of the Maya. Kings and priests carried out religious ceremonies. They also told people when to plant and harvest crops, when to celebrate festivals and how to do most things according to what they said the gods told them. Officials of the king's court made laws and organized building projects. Most of the Maya, however, worked as farmers, using various ways to grow their crops.

Raised beds

Archaeologists studying photographs taken from aircraft have found evidence that some Maya farmers grew crops in raised beds alongside canals. These were raised areas of earth, piled high to stop them being flooded. They piled up **fertile** mud from the bottom of swampy areas and planted crops in it. In the irrigation ditches or canals that ran between the raised beds, farmers even farmed fish to catch and eat.

MAYA CROPS

Maize was the main Maya crop. The Maya also grew beans and squash and a starchy root called manioc or cassava.

FERTILIZING CROPS

The slash-and-burn agriculture used by the Maya is still a widely used method of growing food. The ash left by burning vegetation provides the newly cleared land with a nutrient-rich layer to help fertilize crops.

Slash and burn

Many Maya farmers used slash-and-burn agriculture. They cut down all the trees in an area of the forest and set fire to them. Then they poked sticks into the rich ash left by the fires, and dropped seeds collected from the previous year's crops into the holes. Plants grew well but after two or three years, **nutrients** in the soil ran out and the area needed to be left empty for up to 15 years. So, the farmers then moved on to a new area and repeated the process.

Terraces

Maya people living near mountains dug terraces into the steep hillsides. Terraces are narrow fields that are cut like steps into a hillside and surrounded by a short mud or stone wall. The walls trap water for maize or other crops. The Maya used canals to irrigate terraced crops. They did the same in fields of crops created by slash-and-burn methods.

Arts and crafts

Many ancient Maya made items that graced temples, and the palaces and homes of the rich. The Maya craftsmen used a wide variety of materials to make decorative and useful objects, from death masks to water jugs.

Jewellery and jade

Earlier Maya made pendants and necklaces out of materials such as flint (a type of rock), shell and bone. When they discovered gold and silver, they started to make jewellery from these precious metals. They sometimes used jade to make large chest pendants called pectorals. These pectorals were very precious because they were made from large pieces of jade, and sawing the jade into a thin, flat form would have been very difficult and taken great skill. Precious pectorals such as this were usually worn only on a king's chest during important religious ceremonies.

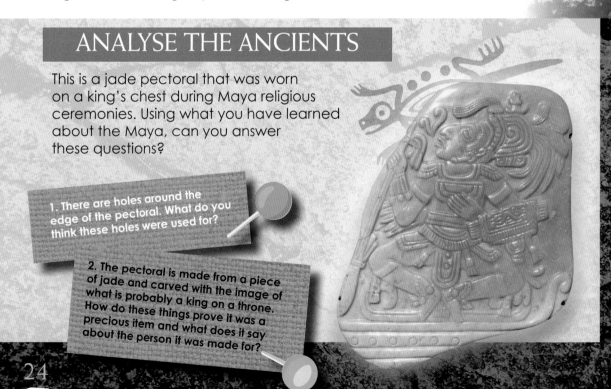

ANALYSE THE ANCIENTS

This is a jade pectoral that was worn on a king's chest during Maya religious ceremonies. Using what you have learned about the Maya, can you answer these questions?

1. There are holes around the edge of the pectoral. What do you think these holes were used for?

2. The pectoral is made from a piece of jade and carved with the image of what is probably a king on a throne. How do these things prove it was a precious item and what does it say about the person it was made for?

Perfect potters

The Maya were master potters. They created beautiful
vases, plates and pots by coiling rings of clay on top of
each other and smoothing the surface by hand. They
made some pottery artefacts using complex moulds.
Moulds are hollow forms into which something is poured
so it sets in the same shape as the mould, as it dries. Most
types of pottery were brightly painted. The Maya often
covered their ceramics with a fine plaster, called stucco,
then painted them while the clay was still wet. They painted
gods, animals and scenes from everyday life.

Trade and merchants

Trade, the buying and selling of goods, was almost as important as agriculture in making the Maya civilization what it was. Farmers brought their food to markets in the cities to sell, and merchants traded luxury goods and useful items far and wide.

On the move

As well as items made by artists and craftsmen, the Maya traded in feathers, salt, jade, emeralds and other precious stones, gold, honey, animal skins, vegetable dyes, medicines made from plants and dried chilli peppers. The Maya from one city-state exchanged and sold goods to other city-states and with other people as far away as the Caribbean. Maya traders travelled vast distances by sea or river in large canoes. They cut roads and routes through the forests. Trading boats sailed to and from the city of Tulum on the coast. They carried cargoes of products such as copper bells, axes and cotton, but mainly turquoise and jade.

THE CITY OF TULUM

The city of Tulum was built on a 12-metre- (40-foot-) high cliff. It faced the Caribbean Sea and was surrounded by high walls on three sides. The walls were probably to protect it from invaders wanting to steal the valuable goods stored temporarily inside.

Mighty merchants

Merchants were important to Maya culture and were treated with a lot of respect. On artefacts, they are always shown with helpers or slaves, and pictured carrying fans, which are a Maya **symbol** of importance. Merchants even had their own god, Ek Chuah, whom they worshipped every day. The seas they travelled were prone to hurricanes and they risked being attacked by thieves on long trips. So it was important to keep Ek Chuah happy.

Barter and exchange

The Maya did not buy goods with coins. They usually exchanged or bartered goods or services with each other. So, for example, a farmer might give a merchant food in exchange for salt. It was difficult to grow cacao trees and they did not produce many beans each season. So cacao beans were very valuable, and people often used them as payment for goods. Cacao beans were used so often that they became a form of currency (money).

CACAO CURRENCY
Cacao beans became a form of currency because everyone wanted them. People were happy to hand over many types of products in exchange for the precious beans.

CHAPTER 5

Maya inventions

The Maya used many of the **resources** from the natural world around them to make some new and useful inventions. They cut stone from rocks, and used wood from the rainforest trees they cut down when clearing land for farming and building.

Reservoirs

The Maya also invented vast underground **reservoirs** that held fresh water to help people survive times of drought. To make the reservoirs, they cleared large sections of the rainforest to build artificial underground lakes where fresh water could be collected and stored. Archaeologists have discovered that the Maya lined these huge reservoirs with broken pieces of pottery and ceramics. A similar practice is used to line swimming pools today. The reservoirs were large enough to supply whole cities with fresh water in an emergency, such as a drought.

YUCATAN RESERVOIR
This is a Maya water reservoir found underground in Yucatan, Mexico.

Obsidian knives

The Maya discovered that obsidian, a black, glass-like volcanic rock, is one of the sharpest substances found in nature. They carved it into knives used in sacrificial surgery. Certain priests acted as doctors and used the knives to perform operations. The knives cut very neatly, which helped scars heal faster. Obsidian is still used today in some hospitals to perform heart by-pass surgeries.

Weapons of war

Maya warriors invented a type of tear gas, used to irritate people's eyes, nose and throat, and to make them cry, sneeze and cough. The Maya tear gas was made by burning chilli peppers and blowing the smoke towards the enemy. While enemy warriors were struggling to see, the Maya could attack them.

The Maya also invented a type of bomb using gourds. A gourd is a large fruit with a hard skin. The Maya emptied the shell of a gourd and filled it with wasps and bees, then flung it at their enemies.

Cool calculators!

The Maya had sophisticated systems for counting, tracking time and marking important times of the year. They studied the skies from their observatories, mapped the movements of the Sun, Moon, planets and stars, and used their discoveries to create three calendars.

Keeping track of time

The Maya used calendars to plan religious ceremonies, wars and harvests. The Tzolk'in calendar lasted 260 days, and each day had a name and number. The Haab calendar was a 365-day calendar, like the one used today. It had 19 months, however: 18 with 20 days, and 1 with 5 unlucky days. A special Long Count calendar was used to measure very long periods of time.

ALL IN THE STARS!
Chichen Itza was an important Maya observatory. The Maya used it to track the movement of the planet Venus. Depending on where the planet was in the sky, they would wage war on their enemies!

ANALYSE THE ANCIENTS

Take a look at this Maya calendar. Based on the information you have learned, can you answer the questions to analyse the Maya?

1. The symbols around the edge of the calendar represent months. Why do you think it was so important for the Maya to track the seasons and time?

2. The calendar gave the Maya a way of structuring their year. How do you think this may have helped their civilization to develop?

Keeping count

The Maya developed a counting system that was widely used more than 2,000 years before mathematics was common in Europe. Not only that, but they also used the concept of zero more than 1,000 years before any other culture. They used their counting systems for many things, from buying and selling in the market to keeping track of calendar events and predicting **eclipses** of the Sun and Moon.

Instead of counting in tens, the ancient Maya used a counting system based on 20. This means that instead of counting 1, 10, 100, 1,000 and 10,000, the Maya used 1, 20, 400, 8,000 and 160,000. Instead of many different numbers, their counting system used just three symbols in several different combinations:
• a dot represented 1
• a bar or stick represented 5
• a shell represented 0.

Maya hieroglyphs

In around 250 BC, the Maya developed the first system of writing in the Americas. Like the ancient Egyptians, they used hundreds of symbols called hieroglyphs that represented words, ideas, syllables or sounds.

Deciphering the code

It took archaeologists a long time to decipher (work out) the Maya hieroglyphs and what they meant. There are 800 different hieroglyphs and the system is quite complicated. Some of the hieroglyphs are pictures that represent what something means, but others showed readers how to sound out a word. The Maya writing system fully represented their spoken languages. It was the only **Mesoamerican** writing system to do so.

Stories of the scribes

The Maya who carved hieroglyphs into stone monuments or painted them on pottery or cloth were known as scribes. While only people of the upper caste were educated enough to fully read and write, it is likely that many Maya could read or recognize the public writings on walls and monuments. The job of a scribe was not just to write down facts. He worked for the king and nobles, so it was his job to make the king sound as wonderful and powerful as possible to keep the people of the city-states loyal to their leaders.

PICTURE WRITING
Most of the Maya hieroglyphs are in the form of pictures that represent real objects such as animals, people and objects from daily life.

Secrets in the codices

One of the most valuable sources of evidence of Maya history that we have comes from their codices. These are folding books made of paper from the bark of fig trees and covered in white lime. Originally, they were bound in jaguar skins. The codices were used to set dates for religious rituals and information, often by linking them to **astronomical** events. For example, many pages show a god and describe what that god is doing. Many other pages contain lists of numbers that allowed the Maya to predict eclipses, the phases of the Moon and the movements of the planets.

CHAPTER 6

Everyday life

In Maya culture, the sort of day-to-day life you lived depended on which caste you were born into. If your father was a farmer, you became a farmer when you grew up, too. You lived a very different life from the people in the castes above you.

Kings, priests and nobles

Kings, priests and nobles lived a life of luxury. They had servants and slaves. Peasants brought the powerful priests tributes (gifts). Peasants also worked for them for free, doing whatever the priests needed. The lives of the rich and powerful were so different from that of ordinary people, that most people only saw them at festivals. Some nobles had jobs working as officials, scribes, military leaders or in business and trade. But even they had a great deal of free time and lived lives of luxury.

CARVED COLUMN
This carved column shows a warrior with two attendants. Only important people had monuments of themselves made in stone like this.

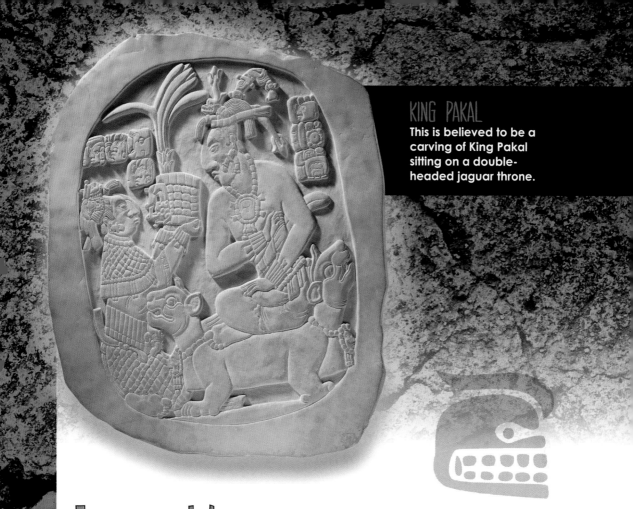

Farmers and slaves

Ordinary people worked very hard almost every day. The men were mostly farmers and the women looked after the home, children and garden. They woke up early after a night of sleeping on reed mats, and said a prayer at the family shrine in their one-room home. They then worked all day, and stopped only when it grew dark. Ordinary people were expected to do as they were told and stay in their own areas. They were not allowed to speak directly to a noble. If they wanted to ask something, they had to speak to one of the noble's servants and the servant passed on the message.

Slaves were not free to come and go as they pleased, but they were not usually treated poorly. In some cases, their lives were easier than a farmer's, depending on who their masters were and what job they were given to do.

Maya style

The Maya took a lot of pride in the way they looked. They wanted to please the gods, show off their social status and look good. They pierced their ears, noses and lips, had patterns and symbols tattooed into their skin and filed their teeth into points. They even went so far as to bind their babies' heads so they grew long, flat foreheads. They thought this made people look more like gods. The richer and more powerful they were, the more body decorations they had.

Feathers and finery

Kings, priests and nobles drilled holes in their teeth into which they put pieces of jade, turquoise or other precious stones. They wore large jade earplugs in their ears. At festivals, they wore lavish outfits to show off how important they were. They wore their fine jewellery and tall headdresses made from the colourful feathers of rare birds, which were sometimes as tall as the people wearing them. They wore clothing made from the skins of animals such as jaguars. Jaguars were the most dangerous predators in the Maya jungles. The king often wore jaguar skins as a symbol of his power.

ANALYSE THE ANCIENTS

This vase has an image of the Maya royal court. Read all of the information on these two pages, then use it to help you answer the questions below.

1. This figure is wearing a headdress made of feathers. What does this tell us about who they were and how important they were?

2. The figure is sitting on jaguar skins. Why were these used to show how important someone was?

Simple clothes

Ordinary people wore simple outfits. Men wore a type of short skirt, called a loincloth, and cotton turbans. Women wore a long skirt and a loose tunic shirt woven from cotton or other plant fibres. Outfits often included colourful woven and **embroidered** belts, sashes, scarves and headbands. Both men and women wore jewellery made from materials such as bone, sticks or clay. In winter, they wore an embroidered cape to keep warm. There were laws to stop them wearing feathers in their hair or the tall headdresses that the nobles wore. If ordinary people tried to behave or dress like a noble, the penalty could be death.

Feasts and food

You may not realize it, but the Maya created some of our favourite foods. They also ate some types of food that most of us would probably avoid today!

The first drinking chocolate

The Maya were the first people to use the seeds from cacao trees. They roasted and ground cacao beans and mixed them with water and spices to make a bitter-tasting chocolate drink that they called *xocoatl*. This was a very early version of the hot chocolate that people drink today, although we tend to have it with sugar and milk. For the Maya, cacao was a sacred gift of the gods. Mostly only royalty and nobles could afford to drink xocoatl.

THE DRINK OF THE GODS
The Maya called drinking chocolate the drink of the gods. Nobles had special drinking vessels, such as this one, made for drinking it.

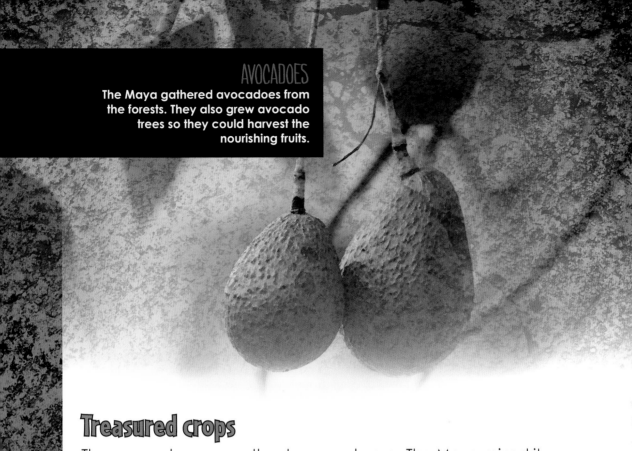

Treasured crops

The avocado was another treasured crop. The Maya mixed it with chillis, garlic, coriander, onions and lime or lemon, to make delicious guacamole. Maize was such an important food to the Maya that they believed the gods first created people from masa (maize dough). They ate maize as corn on the cob, used it to make a kind of porridge for breakfast and ground up kernels to make a thin, flat bread called tortilla, which they ate with every meal. One food they enjoyed that we do not eat today is insects. The Maya fried maguey worms and other insects, and wrapped them in tortillas to take to the fields for a tasty lunch.

A varied diet

The Maya grew a lot of fruit and vegetables. They also hunted, fished and gathered wild foods, so they had a varied diet. They ate squash, tomatoes, peppers, pineapples, papayas and cactus fruits such as prickly pears. They used bows and arrows to hunt iguanas, frogs, snakes, deer, rabbits and pig-like animals called peccary. They also ate shellfish such as oysters.

Ball games

Regular religious festivals and celebrations broke up the endless days of hard work. One of the most popular events was a ball game. This was far more serious than the games played today because each game had religious significance and the team that lost was usually sacrificed!

The importance of the games

The Maya ball game represented a struggle between gods of the day and night, or the sky and the underworld. The ball was a symbol of the Sun, Moon or stars, and the rings represented sunrise and sunset. Ball games went on for days and were attended by thousands of people. Kings and priests carried out rituals before and after the game, and there was music and singing. The winners of the game were treated as heroes and given a great feast. Like many of the Maya celebrations, these events made people feel as though they belonged to an important and long-lasting culture.

BALL-COURT RUINS

These are the ruins of a ball court in the Maya site of Ek Balam (meaning "black jaguar"), now in Yucatan, Mexico.

Playing the game

The Maya built huge stone ball courts on which to play the game. The largest ever found was at Chichen Itza and it measured 168 metres (550 feet) by 70 metres (230 feet). Most ball courts had two sloping walls opposite each other. High up on the walls were three round disks called markers or a single stone ring. There were two teams, and players scored points by touching the markers or passing a heavy, hard rubber ball, which weighed more than 900 grams (2 pounds), through the ring. The players could touch and pass the ball to each other using only their elbows, knees or hips, but never their hands or feet.

The players wore a horseshoe-shaped yoke around their waist and padding over their knees and elbows to reduce injury from the ball. Images of the ball game on painted pottery suggest that players wore different headdresses to show which team they belonged to.

SHOOTING HOOPS

It was very difficult to get the ball through the stone hoop, so players rarely scored. Games often ended after one team finally got the ball through.

41

The end of the Maya

Why the mighty Maya culture suddenly collapsed some time during the eighth or ninth century is a mystery. Experts have different ideas about why this civilization came to an end and why, within about 100 years, the busy cities turned to empty ruins.

Decline of the city-states

Some experts think that there may have been an epidemic (deadly disease) that passed through the Maya cities and wiped out many of its people. At some Maya sites, the bodies found within mass graves suggest the victims met a violent end. This suggests that their cities were attacked and they were killed in battle. Others speculate that after years of slashing and burning the area, the land was no longer fertile and good for growing crops. If a drought happened at a time when there were fewer crops, many Maya would have starved. Survivors might have fled the cities to make a new life elsewhere.

KINGLY STELA

This is a stela, a tall stone slab covered with an image of a king and details about his life and achievements. The kings ordered stelae made to show their achievements so they would be remembered. These monuments are still important records of Maya history today.

Lost in time

When Spanish explorers arrived in the region, some religious leaders burned all but four of the Maya codices, which might have held the answers to the mystery of what happened to the Maya. Luckily, the Maya made many of their buildings and artefacts from stone and engraved names, dates and stories on some of them. Although the wind and rain, and people who came to the area later, have damaged these buildings, they have still provided us with a lot of information about the incredible Maya culture.

THE LAST MAYA CITY

Mayapan was the last great Maya city. It was surrounded by a wall 9 kilometres (5.6 miles) long, which may suggest that the later Maya were threatened with attack from outsiders.

Did you manage to analyse the ancients?
Check against the answers on these pages.

PAGE 9

1. The battle scene shows that, contrary to what people once believed, the Maya were not an altogether peaceful people and that there were often violent battles between city-states.
2. Wooden spear poles rot away, but images such as the one on page 9 show wooden spear poles with stone tips. This helps archaeologists to identify the artefacts they find.

PAGE 11

1. The building at the top of the pyramid was used as a temple to worship the Maya gods.
2. The pyramid and temple are high for several reasons: to bring priests and kings close to the gods, to remind people that the gods were always watching over them and so people could use the pyramids as landmarks.

PAGE 18

1. The Maya believed the underworld was connected to the sea and conch shells come from the sea, which made them linked to the underworld.
2. The fact that conch shells come from the sea makes them rare and valuable to cities far inland among the forests.

PAGE 24

1. The holes around the edge of the pectoral would have had string threaded through them so the item could be worn hanging over the chest.
2. Jade was very precious, rare and difficult to work with, so only important people wore large, intricate pieces such as the pectoral shown on page 24. The image of the king suggests a king would have worn it for special ceremonies.

ANSWERS

PAGE 31

1. The Maya used calendars to plan religious ceremonies, wars and harvests.
2. The use of calendars allowed the Maya to track time and develop a sophisticated society that could organize itself well.

PAGE 36

1. Only kings and important people wore tall headdresses. Common people were punished if they did so.
2. Jaguars were the most dangerous predators in the Maya jungles, so having their skins suggested to people that kings were even more powerful.

GLOSSARY

afterlife life after death

ancestors relatives who have died

aqueduct artificial channel for carrying water

architects people who design and plan buildings

astronomical to do with the planets and other objects in space

bloodletting cutting the skin to let out a small amount of blood

city-states cities that with their surrounding areas form an independent state

civilization settled and stable community in which people live together peacefully and use systems such as writing to communicate

culture beliefs, customs and arts of a particular group of people or country

eclipses times when the Sun is hidden by the Moon or the Moon is hidden by Earth's shadow

embroidered decorated with stitches made by sewing

fertile describes soil that is full of nutrients so plants grow well in it

inherited receive from one's parents

Mesoamerican of or relating to the region of Mexico and central America where the Maya lived

nobles people of the highest class in certain societies

nutrients substances that plants and animals need to be healthy and to grow well

offerings gifts that people give as part of a religious ceremony or ritual

pyramids large structures built with a square base and four triangular sides meeting at a point at the top

quarry place where stone or other minerals are dug from the ground

reservoirs artificial lakes for collecting and storing water

resources things, such as water and rock, that can be used or made into new things

rituals ceremonies performed for religious reasons

sacred special or important to a religion

sacrificed killed to honour a god or gods

slaves people who are owned by other people and have to obey them

symbol image that represents something else

tapestries large fabric pictures made by embroidery

temples buildings where people go to worship their god or gods

tombs buildings where dead people are put to rest

Books

Daily Life in the Maya Civilization (Daily Life in Ancient Civilizations), Nick Hunter (Raintree, 2016)

DKfindout! Maya, Incas and Aztecs, DK (DK Children, 2018)

Mayan Civilization (Explore!), Izzi Howell (Wayland, 2018)

The Maya (Great Civilizations), Tracey Kelly (Frankliin Watts, 2015)

The Mayans (History Hunters), Louise Spilsbury (Raintree, 2016)

Websites

www.bbc.com/bitesize/articles/zg2htv4
Learn what life was like for the Maya.

www.dkfindout.com/uk/history/mayans
Find out more about the Maya.

INDEX